Withdrawn From
Circulation

BETH TFILOH LIBRARY
3300 Old Court Rd.
Baltimore, MD 21208

TIMELINES

1910s

by
Gail B. Stewart

BETH TFILOH LIBRARY
3300 Old Court Rd.
Baltimore, MD 21208

CRESTWOOD HOUSE
New York

Library of Congress Cataloging In Publication Data
Stewart, Gail, 1949-
 1910s / by Gail B. Stewart.
 p. cm. — (Timelines)
 Includes index.
 Summary: History, trivia, and fun through photographs and articles present life
in the United States from 1910-1919.
 ISBN 0-89686-472-3
 1. History, Modern—20th century—Miscellanea—Juvenile literature. [1. United
States—History—1909-1913—Miscellanea. 2. United States—History—1913-1921—
Miscellanea.] I. Title. II. Series.
D422.S78   1989   973.91'2—dc20   89-9946
                                                          CIP
                                                          AC

Photo credits
Cover: Planters Life Savers Company: An advertisement for Life Savers candy during
    World War I
Wide World Photos: 4, 6, 7, 16, 18, 19, 20, 30, 35, 38, 41, 46
FPG International: 9, 11, 12, 25, 27, 29, 33, 34, 36, 40, 43
The Bettmann Archive: 15, 22, 23, 28, 45

Copyright © 1989 by Crestwood House, Macmillan Publishing Company

All rights reserved. No part of this book may be reproduced or transmitted in
any form or by any means, electronic or mechanical, including photocopying,
recording, or by any information storage and retrieval system, without
permission in writing from the Publisher.

Macmillan Publishing Company
866 Third Avenue
New York, NY 10022
Collier Macmillan Canada, Inc.

CRESTWOOD HOUSE

Produced by Carnival Enterprises

Printed in the United States of America

First Edition

10 9 8 7 6 5 4 3 2 1

CONTENTS

INTRODUCTION

America in 1910 was still mainly a nation of farms and small towns. However, that was beginning to change. As the decade progressed, Americans began to leave the farms. They were moving to the cities—especially Northern cities like Chicago and New York—to work in factories. Blacks, or African-Americans, moved in the greatest numbers. This was because they were often discriminated against in the rural South.

During this decade, America joined the world in the most horrible war ever imagined. World War I was complete with fighter airplanes, poison gas, and machine guns.

But this was also a time of great inventions, of pushing the bounds of "what might be" into "what is." Kids were enjoying bicycles, pogo sticks, and sleds. They also loved the latest movie —*Tarzan of the Apes.*

Madame Marie Curie won the Nobel Prize for chemistry in 1911.

5

The uncomfortable hobble skirt

"IDIOTIC" SKIRTS

A very strange kind of skirt became fashionable in 1910. It was full at the hips but tapered to a very narrow opening at the ankles. It was called the "hobble skirt," for any woman wearing one had to hobble when she walked!

Traffic in New York and Chicago came to a standstill many times. Why? Many "hobbling" women, bouncing along like birds, tried unsuccessfully to cross streets before the lights changed!

Calling the fashion "idiotic," members of the Illinois State Legislature outlawed the skirt. They claimed that women who wore hobble skirts were putting themselves in danger of falling or causing general confusion in public places!

TOAST IN EVERY ROOM

Up until 1910, when people wanted their bread toasted, they had to stoke up the fire, put the bread in a metal holder with a long handle, and dangle the bread in the fire.

The invention of electricity changed this and many other household appliances. The first electric toaster, made in 1910, looked like a metal skeleton of a modern toaster. There were no

Samuel Langhorne Clemens

controls, no outside covers—all the coils and wires were exposed.

The real selling point wasn't the beauty of the toaster but the convenience. One didn't have to get a fire going in the kitchen stove just to make a slice of toast. In fact, one of the first advertisements for the toaster urged people to get one for every room.

A BELOVED AMERICAN DIES

Samuel Langhorne Clemens, who wrote under the name Mark Twain, died on April 21. Clemens was well known as the author of *The Adventures of Tom Sawyer* and *Huckleberry Finn* and other novels about growing up in small-town Missouri. Clemens was 74 when he died.

1910

SODA FOUNTAIN BLUES

In 1910, many kinds of soft drinks were popular, but a new one called Dr Pepper was really catching on.

The drink was invented by a soda jerk, a person who worked behind the counter in a drugstore making sodas, malts, and other treats. He loved to put different flavors of syrup together as experiments. His boss, Dr. Pepper, didn't approve of the boy's hobby. Dr. Pepper also didn't approve of the boy's interest in Pepper's daughter!

One day the boss had enough of the lovestruck soda jerk with all his exotic concoctions. He fired the boy, who soon left for Texas to make his fortune.

But old habits die hard, and the young man ended up in a Texas drugstore making his flavorful inventions. One particular combination was extremely popular, and he marketed it. The name he chose was that of his old boss—Dr Pepper.

THE LAST LAUGH

An Indiana man named S. H. Schrapp laughed uncontrollably for more than 12 hours on November 8, 1910.

What started him off? Apparently Schrapp had convinced another farmer to buy a mule, thinking it was a horse. The whole idea amused Schrapp so much he began to chuckle, then to giggle, and finally to laugh.

At first the laughter seemed harmless, but after it had continued for more than an hour, neighbors summoned a doctor. The doctor tried everything he could think of to stop the laughter. Nothing worked. Finally, at the 12-hour-mark, another doctor gave Schrapp a large electric shock, and he stopped laughing. As far as anyone knows, that was the longest laugh in history.

Jack Johnson won boxing's world heavyweight title in 1910.

RACIAL TROUBLES IN THE RING

On the Fourth of July a black boxer named Jack Johnson beat Jim Jeffries, a white man. The fight was important, for it determined the world heavyweight title. It was important in another way, for it showed how prejudiced many whites were at that time.

Race riots erupted in many parts of the country. A white man was attacked by other whites simply because he had rooted for Johnson. Altogether at least eleven people were killed in such incidents.

FACTORY FIRE KILLS 141

A fire swept through a New York dressmaking factory on March 25, and killed 141 people. The fire is known as the Triangle Shirtwaist Fire. Most of the victims were Jewish or Italian immigrants—many were under the age of 16 and were working for extremely low wages.

The fire escape doors were locked, to prevent employees and outsiders from stealing. The attention the fire brought helped bring about changes in working conditions.

DON'T CROSS THAT LINE!

It was in 1911 that the first painted lines appeared on a road. The lines were not drawn by a highway department, or by the government, as you might expect. Instead, a Michigan man named Edward Hines painted the white lines by hand on River Road in Trenton, Michigan. He was tired of all the automobile drivers who didn't have enough sense to stay on one side of the road or the other.

Evidently, the lines worked. In the next several years, white lines were painted on roads in cities and counties all over the country.

WHERE'S THAT SMILE?

The most famous painting in the world was stolen on August 22 from the Louvre in Paris. The *Mona Lisa* was a portrait of a young woman with a mysterious smile, by Leonardo da Vinci. The theft happened in the middle of the night. The *Mona Lisa* had hung in the Louvre for 400 years and was considered a national treasure of France.

The Mona Lisa *is safely returned to the Louvre in Paris, two years after its theft in 1911.*

Authorities were puzzled. Who would steal such a well-known painting? Surely the thief couldn't sell it. Everyone would know it was stolen! Police and art experts throughout the world guessed that whoever did it was simply crazy.

It wasn't until two years later that police recovered the painting. The thief had tried to return the portrait to Italy, where da Vinci had painted it. Instead, he was arrested immediately. Within a week "the lady with the mysterious smile" was back at the Louvre.

1911

VITAMINS NAMED

Casimir Funk, a research scientist in Germany, wondered what was in certain foods that made them nutritious or not. Funk studied a diet for pigeons. He isolated a tiny element in rice that was necessary for the birds to stay healthy.

He decided to call the element "vitamin." The Latin word *vita* means "life." Funk was sure that every healthful food must have some form of vitamin.

NEW TOOL FOR POLICE

Police were given fresh help in catching the bad guys when in 1911 someone found a way of gathering fingerprints at the scene of a crime.

The first case in which the new system was tried involved a

burglar named "Charlie Crispi" Cella. His fingerprints were gathered by police officers, and he was convicted. Tough luck, Charlie!

CHEVROLET OPENS FACTORY

A Swiss-born American named Louis Chevrolet had an announcement in November. He was going to open an automobile factory in Detroit. His goal: to manufacture expensive touring cars.

Chevrolet had a reputation as a daring driver himself. In 1905 he had won a race in New York, achieving the unbelievably fast speed of 68 miles per hour.

A HIGH HONOR

Madame Marie Curie won the Alfred Nobel prize for chemistry in 1911. She was the first person in history to win the honored prize twice.

Marie was from Poland and met her husband while studying in France. They won the award for physics in 1903, for their work with radioactivity. After Pierre Curie was killed in an accident in 1906, Marie continued her experiments. Her 1911 award was for isolating two important chemical elements: radium and polonium.

THE BOTTOM OF THE WORLD

A Norwegian expedition led by Roald Amundsen was the first ever to reach the South Pole. On December 14, five people planted the Norwegian flag at "the bottom of the world."

Amundsen's expedition had been racing against a British expedition led by Robert Scott. Many thought Scott's group would arrive first because they were using a combination of ponies and motorized vehicles. Amundsen's group relied on old-fashioned dog sleds for transportation and won.

A method of collecting fingerprints at the scene of a crime was discovered in 1911. A few years later, a Los Angeles detective devised a way of enlarging the prints.

"ANGEL OF THE BATTLEFIELD" DEAD AT 90

Clara Barton died on April 12, 1912. She had gained world-wide respect as the founder of the American Red Cross.

A nurse during the American Civil War, Barton often risked her life to care for the wounded. She became interested in nursing, she once said, when she was a child and had provided around-the-clock care for her brother, David, after he had fallen from a barn roof.

Clara Barton grew up in a world with very different ideas about medicine than we have today. Doctors and nurses often used leeches to suck blood out of sick people. They believed the worms could drain out the poisons that caused illness. Clara Barton lived at a time when women were often treated as though they were ignorant and useless. Even though she showed great courage and resourcefulness in her work, some of her male co-workers still called her "a pest in petticoats."

THE "UNSINKABLE" TITANIC

The owners of the *Titanic* were very proud of their new ocean liner. They pointed to the ship's beautiful rooms and elegant dining facilities. They called it "the ultimate luxury liner." They also bragged that the boat was "unsinkable." Nevertheless, on April 15, during its maiden (first) voyage, the *Titanic* sank. The ship hit an iceberg that ripped a 300-foot hole in its side and it went down in the North Atlantic. More than 1,500 people were drowned.

For all its beauty and elegance, the *Titanic* lacked enough lifeboats for all the people on board. Of the 2,224 who boarded in England for the trip to New York, only 711 survived.

The disaster did result in better laws, however. All steamships immediately were required to carry enough lifeboats and rafts for everybody on board.

14

This painting shows the terrified survivors watching the sinking of the Titanic.

PICTURE POSTCARD CRAZE

The latest collectible was a colorful picture postcard. You could buy one for a penny—of almost anything. Cats, dogs, buildings, cars—you name the subject, it was probably on a penny postcard.

The cards were passed around and admired, or traded for more interesting ones. The largest picture postcard collection on record belonged to a boy from Ohio. He had 73,455 of them. Historians say that the craze died out as photography got more popular. After people began having their own cameras, they took pictures of their families and friends and passed those around.

GIRL SCOUTS BEGIN

In 1912, an American woman named Juliette Low returned from England and brought the idea of Girl Scouts with her.

While living in London, Low had met Colonel Robert Baden-Powell, the founder of the Boy Scouts. She felt a similar organi-

Girl Scout founder Juliette Low (far right) salutes the flag with the first Girl Scout troop.

zation for young girls would be successful. It could encourage them to help others and improve their communities.

Low began a troop of Girl Scouts in her hometown of Savannah, Georgia. There were 18 in that first troop. By the time of her death just 15 years later, more than 140,000 girls belonged to the Girl Scouts nationwide. Today, more than three million girls belong to Scout troops.

CONES MADE FASTER

Ever since the invention of the ice-cream cone, cones had been rolled individually by hand. In 1912 an inventor named Frederick Bruckman created a machine that could do the job in a second or two.

48 STARS ON THE FLAG!

Arizona became the 48th state in 1912. At first, President Taft denied statehood to Arizona. Its constitution allowed for something Taft didn't like. Arizona lawmakers wanted judges recalled if the people felt they were doing a poor job. But Taft felt that a judge should be above politics.

Arizona dropped the recall idea from its constitution, and Taft agreed to grant statehood. (Once Arizona was officially a state, its legislature put back the recall of judges amendment!)

THE CANDY WITH THE HOLE

In 1912 a new kind of candy hit the market. Sold in a roll, each piece was the size of a dime. The candy was unique because it had a hole in the middle.

They were called Life Savers because of their shape. And they came in one flavor—mint. The 1913 package had a picture of a sailor throwing a life saver to a swimming lady, with the words: "Life Savers—for that stormy breath."

A roll of Life Savers cost a nickel.

1913

FIRST GAS STATION

Although automobiles had been around for several years, gas stations were unheard of. People purchased the fuel they needed at general stores, in the same way as they bought kerosene for their lamps.

In 1913, the first drive-in gas station opened in Pittsburgh. It was owned by the Gulf Company and was open 24 hours a day. The manager reported that the first day was a good beginning. He sold 30 gallons of gas!

A NEW PRESIDENT

Woodrow Wilson was inaugurated as the 28th president of the United States in March. He had defeated the president in office, William Howard Taft.

The world's first drive-in gas station opened in Pittsburgh.

Woodrow Wilson takes the oath of office to become the 28th president of the United States.

A quiet man, Wilson had been governor of New Jersey before running for president. His election marked the first time in 20 years that a Democrat had been voted into the White House.

A SURPRISE INSIDE

The candied peanuts and popcorn snack Cracker Jack had been around since 1893. But 1913 was the first year that the company began putting a small toy in the box!

The inventor of the snack was a German immigrant named F. W. Rueckheim. He chose the name because "crackerjack" was a slang term for "great" or "fantastic." The little boy pictured on the label was Rueckheim's grandson, who died of pneumonia at the age of eight.

New automobiles travel on an assembly line at the Ford Motor Company's factory in Highland Park, Michigan.

BUILDING THEM FASTER

In 1913, automobile maker Henry Ford decided to change the way his company built cars. Borrowing an idea from meat packers, he began using conveyor belts, which moved the car down an assembly line. Along the way, different workers added parts to the car until it was completed.

This turned out to be a good idea for the company and the consumer. Ford began making 1,000 cars a day, and he was able to charge much less for each car. Car buyers paid $850 for the Model T when it was first introduced. A 1913 model cost only $260!

Workers at Ford's assembly line were happy, too—he raised their salaries to an unheard-of $5 per week.

NOT AN AMATEUR

On January 27 Jim Thorpe announced that he had played professional baseball before the 1912 Olympics. That meant that he was not an amateur athlete. He was, therefore, ineligible for the Olympics.

The news stunned sports fans everywhere, for Jim Thorpe was considered the best athlete in the world. He had won both the Decathlon and Pentathlon trophies. No one else had ever come close.

The Olympics have always been for amateurs—those who have never been paid to play sports. Thorpe sadly returned the trophies to the Olympic Committee.

ZIP IT UP!

Sometimes we think of certain everyday things as having been around forever. The zipper is one of them. But it wasn't invented until 1913!

An American named Gideon Sundback came out with a zipper, which he called a "hookless fastener." Zippers were first used on tobacco pouches and boots. Nobody was crazy about using them on clothing, since they rusted so easily. When zippers were tried as fasteners for pants and dresses, people had to remove them before washing the clothes and then sew them in again!

The name "zipper" was first used by B. F. Goodrich, who developed a rubber boot with the hookless fastener in 1923. He thought the sound of the fastener closing made a "z-z-zip" sound.

1914

TWO NOTORIOUS GUNSHOTS

On June 28, Austrian Archduke Francis Ferdinand and his wife, Sophie, were assassinated as they were riding in a parade. The gunman was from Serbia, a tiny province just south of Austria-Hungary.

This tragedy was just the beginning. Historians say that Europe was like a powder keg ready to explode. All the major countries in Europe were competing for colonies. Each wanted more power.

A month after the archduke and his wife were gunned down, Austria declared war on Serbia, and World War I began.

When it was all over in 1918, more than nine million soldiers were dead, and the destruction in Europe had been immeasurable.

Austrian Archduke Francis Ferdinand and his wife one hour before they were assassinated

HEIR TO AUSTRIA'S THRONE IS SLAIN WITH HIS WIFE BY A BOSNIAN YOUTH TO AVENGE SEIZURE OF HIS COUNTRY

Francis Ferdinand Shot During State Visit to Sarajevo.

TWO ATTACKS IN A DAY

Archduke Saves His Life First Time by Knocking Aside a Bomb Hurled at Auto.

SLAIN IN SECOND ATTEMPT

Lad Dashes at Car as the Royal Couple Return from Town Hall and Kills Both of Them.

LAID TO A SERVIAN PLOT

Heir Warned Not to Go to Bosnia, Where Populace Met Him with S—

Archduke Francis Ferdinand and his Consort the Duchess of Hohenberg

Slain by Assassin's Bullets.

could only certify they were both dead. The authors of both attacks upon —hduke are born Bosnians. Da— —ssitor, and worked

by splinters from the bomb. Several persons on the pavement were very seriously hurt by the explosion of the bomb, which was thrown by a young— man named Tabri— vics i

It is feared that it will lead to serious complications with that— dom, and m—

The New York Times *reported the assassination of the Austrian archduke and his wife.*

OUT IN THE OPEN: ODO-RO-NO

Although Americans knew all about sweat and odor, it wasn't until 1914 that an antiperspirant company dared to advertise. Before this time people bought deodorants and antiperspirants, but reluctantly. It was too embarrassing.

The product that changed things was Odo-Ro-No, and it claimed to keep people free of perspiration. The ads were aimed strictly at women, promising Odo-Ro-No would keep them dainty and clean.

"IT KNOCKED MY ECZEMA!"

In 1914 a druggist named George Bunting was busy experimenting with a new sunburn ointment. Bathing suits were getting shorter and more revealing. They were short enough to show a little calf, although not a knee! So more skin was being exposed to sunburn.

1914

When he wasn't busy with customers, Dr. Bunting blended ingredients in an old coffeepot and poured the remedy into little blue jars.

He called his product Dr. Bunting's Sunburn Remedy. One day a customer said "Boy, that stuff really knocked my eczema!" Eczema is a condition of dry, scaly skin. Dr. Bunting combined "knocked" and "eczema" and gave his product a new name—Noxzema.

A 48-POUND BABY CHICK?

The parents of a little girl named May Pierstorff wanted to send her to visit her grandmother. Although May and her grandmother lived in the same state (Idaho), they lived so far apart they didn't get to see each other much.

Transportation between their homes was expensive, too expensive for May's parents. Even though May was only four years old, her train ticket still cost full price. Sadly, they were about to break the news to May that she would not be able to see her grandmother that summer, when they thought of something. How about the mail?

Mailing packages was a fairly new idea in 1914. The Pierstorffs weren't sure whether there were regulations about sending a little girl through the mail, but they decided to ask.

The postal clerk looked up rules and regulations in his official book. No packages over 50 pounds were permitted. So far, so good—May was only 48 pounds. Looking further, the clerk read that it was illegal to send lizards through the mail, or insects, or any smelly things. It was, however, permissible to mail baby chicks through the mail.

So the clerk agreed to classify little May as a baby chick. The Pierstorffs paid her postage, all 53 cents of it, and glued the stamps on May's coat. She was loaded into the baggage car of a train. She was delivered to her grandmother's house that night!

Taxpayers line up to pay income tax for the first time.

FIRST INCOME TAX NOT TOO BAD

The U. S. government did not levy a nationwide tax on income—that is, the money a person made by working—until 1914. That first year, only one percent of Americans had to worry about it, and those who did really didn't suffer much. The average for those needing to pay was a mere $41!

LIPSTICK GOES METAL

In 1915, an inventor named Maurice Levy came up with the metal lipstick tube. Before Levy's invention, lipstick was applied by finger or brush from a little glass pot. The metal tube made carrying makeup very fashionable.

When using lipstick, the shape of the lips was more important than color. It was all the rage in 1915 to use lipstick to "paint" on a little "bow" mouth.

BELL CALLS WATSON—LONG DISTANCE!

The inventors of the telephone made another famous call in 1915. But this time, they were a whole country apart. Alexander Graham Bell, whose telephone was the most important invention of 1876, called his assistant Thomas Watson from New York.

Watson was in San Francisco, and the two could hear one another just fine. This was the beginning of transcontinental, or coast-to-coast, phone service.

ASPIRIN INTRODUCED

For centuries people took a medication made from the bark of the willow tree for relief from fevers or arthritis. The drug produced some painful side effects, however, such as stomachaches.

In the late 1800s, a young German named Felix Hoffman began to look for a drug that would ease his father's rheumatism without causing stomach pains. He stumbled onto a drug like the willow tree medicine, only made from a plant called the Spiraea. The drug helped, and people believed it had no side effects!

Hoffman took the formula to his employers, the Bayer Drug Firm in Dusseldorf, Germany. They were excited by the new medicine and decided on a name. The "a" was from "acetyl," the old willow bark medicine. The "spir" was from the Spiraea plant, and the "in" was a common ending for many names of medicines. In 1915, Bayer Aspirin was introduced to the world.

After World War I ended, France, the United States, Britain, and Russia were granted the rights to the trademark of Bayer Aspirin as part of the peace agreement with Germany.

ANYWHERE IN THE CITY FOR A JITNEY

The taxicab industry got started by accident. At first, almost no one really believed that people would *pay* for a ride in an automobile, but as it turned out there were plenty of customers.

The first taxicabs in New York and Chicago would take a passenger anywhere in town for only a "jitney"—a slang term for a nickel. "Jitney" became a common word for the taxi itself in the next decade.

New York City's first taxi fleet

The Lusitania *leaves its dock in New York for the last time.*

LUSITANIA GOES DOWN

On May 7, 1915, a German submarine torpedoed the British passenger ship, *Lusitania.* The incident took place about 12 miles off the shore of Ireland.

Until then, the United States had stayed out of the fierce war raging in Europe. Germany, Austria, and their allies were fighting bitterly against Britain, France, and Russia.

The *Lusitania,* the Germans thought, was carrying war supplies, although the British denied this. The *Lusitania* was hit without warning. After the torpedo struck, the ship tilted so far to one side that it was almost impossible for the passengers and crew to launch the lifeboats. Finally they managed to lower the heavier boats, only to crush many people waiting below.

A second torpedo struck the cargo area of the ship. The *Lusitania* sank under 300 feet of water. Of the 1,959 passengers and crew on board, 1,198 were lost. One hundred and twenty-eight of them were Americans.

This tragic incident eventually led America into joining Britain, Russia, and France against Germany in World War I.

Rescue workers help the survivors of the Lusitania *out of lifeboats.*

1916

WILSON RE-ELECTED

Campaigning on the slogan "He Kept Us Out of War," President Woodrow Wilson won a second term in office. He beat Republican challenger Charles Evans Hughes, but by a very small margin.

NEW IDEAS FOR THE CLASSROOM

In 1916, John Dewey introduced a new theory into schools in the United States. Until then, American education had operated on the theory that every child must know a set body of information.

President Woodrow Wilson is elected to a second term in office.

Dewey said that each child was different. What was important for one child to know wasn't always necessary or practical for another. Why teach a child more arithmetic than he or she will need for a job? argued Dewey. Reading, penmanship, geography — all children had to master these skills and this information, despite their individual needs and interests. This theory is as controversial today as it was then. Are schools teaching the right things? How can we be sure? Who should decide? Educators still wrestle with the questions John Dewey asked.

STRICT RULES FOR TEACHERS

Do you think students have too many rules to follow? Take a look at a few of the rules schoolteachers in West Virginia had to follow:

- Teachers may not travel beyond the city limits unless by permission of the school board.
- Teachers may not date.
- Teachers may not smoke cigarettes.
- Teachers may not dress in bright colors, such as red or orange.

A SAD BEGINNING FOR A FAVORITE DOLL

Marcella Gruelle was a very sick little girl. Her parents tried to find things for her to do as she lay in bed day after day, week after week.

One day, while rummaging around in their attic, her father found an old rag doll. He cleaned it up and gave it to Marcella, who loved it. She named it Raggedy Ann and asked her father to tell her stories about the doll. Her father sat by her bed each afternoon, making up stories about Raggedy Ann and her adventures.

Marcella didn't get well. When she died in 1916, she was still clutching her favorite doll. Her father wanted to preserve the stories they had enjoyed together, so he published them for other children to enjoy. The stories were so popular, in fact, that John Gruelle kept writing more of them—25 in all. Raggedy Ann stories, and the dolls that look just like Marcella's Raggedy Ann, still give pleasure to children all over the world.

TROUBLE WITH PANCHO VILLA

Pancho Villa was not the president of Mexico, but he was eager to start a revolution to overthrow the man who was president, Venustiano Carranza. Pancho Villa had trouble with the United States as well. In March 1916, Villa and his men killed 17 people in New Mexico before riding back across the border. Villa wanted to show Carranza that he could not control northern Mexico.

Furious at Villa's actions and aware that Mexico's President Carranza probably could do little to stop Villa, President Wilson sent General John Pershing and 400 U.S. troops to find Villa. Villa escaped, because he was very popular with people of that region. Pershing's troops did battle with some of Villa's army, but the American soldiers were recalled before Villa was brought to justice.

OPPOSING CHILD LABOR

In 1916 Congress passed a bill that would help put an end to the use of child labor. Some states, especially in the South, still allowed children 12 and 13 years old to work to 14 hours a day in factories and mines.

The new law said children must be at least 16 years old to work in mines and quarries. It provided for an 8-hour work day and a 48-hour work week for minors.

Young mine workers take a lunch break.

THE UNITED STATES ENTERS THE WAR

It was becoming harder and harder for the United States to avoid the war that raged in Europe. The country had been helping the Allies for quite a while, sending supplies to nations fighting Germany.

Since the sinking of the *Lusitania,* President Wilson had insisted Germany promise that such a tragedy would never happen again. However, more and more ships were sunk by German submarines. American ships, all flying neutral flags, were among them.

On April 2, 1917, President Wilson asked Congress to declare war on Germany. Wilson had tried to keep America out of the war. However, the country could no longer hold back. Two days later, on April 4, Congress approved. America was at war.

Soldiers leave for Europe at the start of World War I.

An American soldier throws a hand grenade from his trench in France.

SAVE OUR SAUCEPANS

In 1917, a door-to-door salesman named Edwin Cox had a problem. He had a brand new line of aluminum cookware, but few women wanted to let him in their homes to show it. Cox wished he had some gift, some bonus to offer the customer. Then they might be more willing to give him some business.

Knowing how tough metal pans were to clean, Cox thought about developing a pad that was as tough as steel wool but with soapy cleaner inside. He made the first batch in his kitchen, trimming steel wool into small thick wedges and soaking them in soap. When the pads dried, he soaked them again and again, until they were filled with dry soap.

Cox and his wife tested the stuff out on their own pans, and they were amazed at the results! His wife told him to call it "Save Our Saucepans," or "S.O.S."

Cox loved the name, his customers loved the product, and the little pads are still found in supermarkets today.

1917

THE BLACK SWALLOW OF DEATH

When the United States entered World War I, the War Department made a special announcement to Americans overseas. As of April 1917, any American pilot flying in the French Flying Corps could automatically become an officer if he came back to the U. S. Air Corps. Almost every American flyer who had been helping France was pleased to return as an American

United States pilots during World War I

36

officer. One pilot's request to return was ignored, however.

His name was Eugene Bullard. He was the first black fighter pilot in history. Born a slave in Georgia, Bullard had moved to France because there was less prejudice there.

As a pilot, Bullard was without equal. Known as the "Black Swallow of Death," Bullard earned many medals for his heroic battles in the air. Even so, the United States did not allow him or any black to become an officer. So Bullard flew his missions for France. He continued to earn medals and ribbons, including the coveted *croix de guerre* for extreme bravery.

WOMAN IN THE HOUSE

American women passed another milestone. The first woman elected to Congress began serving her first term in 1917. Her name was Jeannette Rankin, and she was a Republican from Montana.

FULD BROTHERS STRIKE IT RICH

One popular form of entertainment in 1917 was a lap-sized board with the alphabet printed on it. The board came with a small three-sided disk upon which two people placed their fingers. When the people asked the board a question and concentrated, the little disk moved about the board pointing to various letters. The answer would be spelled out, to the delight and astonishment of the players. Was it magic? Could the board really tell the future? No one was sure, but it was fun to think so!

The Ouija Board, as it was called, was introduced by two brothers, William and Isaac Fuld. Although the board had been around a few years, it wasn't until 1917 that it began selling like crazy. Then people bought the board to ask it questions about loved ones in the war: Will my son come back? Is my husband all right? When will my brother be home?

1918

RED BARON SHOT DOWN

On April 22, the infamous Red Baron was shot down and killed. Throughout the war, Germany's ace fighter pilot, Manfred von Richthofen, had been making life miserable for Allied pilots.

No pilot in the war had done as much damage as the Red Baron. Singlehandedly, he had destroyed 80 planes belonging to the Allied air forces.

Although his skill was respected by other pilots, the Red Baron had an arrogant, cocky attitude that many found offensive. When told of the Red Baron's crash, one Allied pilot was quoted as saying, "I hope he roasted all the way down."

U. S. Army Air Corps (later renamed the air force) two-seater used throughout World War I.

AIR MAIL INTRODUCED—SORT OF

May 15, 1918, was to be the first day of a new kind of mail delivery in the United States—air mail. According to plan, President Wilson would introduce the first plane carrying mail in a formal ceremony. The aircraft would take off from a park in Washington, D.C., where thousands of cheering spectators would show their support.

Things didn't work out that way, however. For half an hour the pilot tried frantically to start the plane's engines, but nothing worked. The president and his aides were annoyed. The crowd was restless. It was discovered that there was no gas in the fuel tank!

Once the tank was filled the plane took off, but instead of flying north to his first scheduled stop in Philadelphia, the pilot headed southeast. He made an emergency landing to get directions, and in the process broke his propeller.

The pilot was humiliated. His plane was damaged, and the mail was *not* going through. A truck finally came and took the 140 pounds of mail to Philadelphia. It was not a good beginning!

LIBERTY CABBAGE

Sauerkraut, a popular food made from cabbage, had its name changed for a while in 1918. Since sauerkraut is a German food, and because Americans were very anti-German during the war, the food was renamed "Liberty Cabbage."

The whole idea may sound comical now, but for many Americans who had emigrated to the United States from Germany, these were hard times. Many changed their German-sounding names to more English ones. Schwartz became Short; Mueller became Miller. These German-Americans were afraid they would be considered enemies because they had been born in Germany.

1918

A TERRIBLE WEAPON

As World War I wore on, poison gas was used more and more often. Introduced in 1915 by the German army, the gas could be dropped in bombs by airplanes or shot in cannisters from special guns. The gas was made up of many different chemicals. It was so poisonous that it could kill a person breathing it within minutes.

By 1918, American soldiers relied as much on clumsy gas masks as on their weapons. The gas masks had special air filters made from charcoal. Children in the United States collected peach pits, which were burned to make this charcoal.

Even with the protection of a mask, a soldier could be injured by the gas. Such injuries would make breathing and swallowing painful or cause death. Chemical warfare accounted for 30 percent of all American casualties in World War I. Today, most countries have agreed not to use poison gas.

American soldiers fight in the trenches.

U. S. troops arrive home at the end of World War I for a victory celebration.

A DAY OF REMEMBERING

To celebrate the end of World War I, President Wilson proclaimed November 11, 1919, as Armistice Day. This day, he said, would be important to remind ourselves of the horror of war, and of how grateful the world should be that it was finally over.

At exactly 11 A.M. (the exact time the firing on the battle lines had stopped in 1918), Americans stopped for two minutes of silent prayer. Schools, especially, were involved in Armistice Day. Children were asked to think about loved ones who had come home safely from the war. Many children also thought about those who had never made it home, those who had died in battles overseas.

NEW WAY TO CUT GRASS

Before 1919, people used hand-pushed mowers to cut their lawns. A set of rotary blades twirled faster and faster the harder the mower was pushed. It was a good system, except that the mower seemed to get heavy after a few passes across a yard, and it almost always blistered hands.

In 1919, an American army colonel named Edwin George decided to improve the situation. He attached the gasoline motor from his wife's washing machine to the mower. It worked, and a new product was born.

PROHIBITION BEGINS

On January 29, 1919, the 18th Amendment to the U. S. Constitution became official. It made it illegal to drink, transport, or sell liquor of any sort—including wine and beer.

The 18th Amendment was known as "Prohibition" because it prohibited alcoholic beverages. Liquor was seen as a threat to public health and safety. Liquor was blamed for ruining marriages and breaking up families.

New words were soon added to our vocabulary, such as *speakeasy* (an illegal basement bar), *bootleg* (to smuggle whiskey), and *bathtub gin* (liquor made in the home).

Prohibition remained the law until 1933. At that time it was repealed by popular demand.

During Prohibition, people found all kinds of ways to smuggle alcohol.

STATUE DEDICATED TO INSECT

Alabama farmers dedicated a monument to, of all things, the boll weevil on December 11. The boll weevil was one of the most destructive of all insects, killing millions of dollars worth of cotton plants every year. What on earth would make farmers in one of the nation's top cotton producing areas do such a thing?

Actually, said the farmers, if the boll weevil hadn't been so destructive, they would have continued to grow only cotton. But because it was risky—the insect could wipe out a whole crop—the farmers learned to grow different things. Peanuts, corn, and pecans could thrive in the rich soil, too.

So farmers in 1919 were earning three times the income they made when they grew only cotton. The monument was to thank the boll weevil for teaching them to grow other crops.

RACIAL HATRED AT A BEACH IN CHICAGO

In July, a black boy was swimming at one of Chicago's many beaches along Lake Michigan. He was holding on to a piece of wood and paddling, not watching where he was drifting.

All of a sudden he saw that he had drifted into water facing a beach reserved for whites only. Several white swimmers began to throw rocks at him as he tried to paddle back to the "black" beach.

But he lost a grip on the wood he was using for support. No one knows whether he was hit by a rock and knocked out, or if he became exhausted. Whatever the cause, the boy drowned, and his tragic death set off violence in Chicago.

At first, blacks stormed over to the white beach and fighting broke out there. Later, groups of whites drove into black neighborhoods and fired guns at anyone they could find. For ten days, the city suffered bombings, fires, shootings, and ugly words. When it was all over, 37 people were dead and almost 600 were wounded.

44

FIRST TRIPLE CROWN WINNER

Horse-racing history was made this year at the Belmont Racetrack in Elmont, New York. Sir Barton won the Belmont Stakes and became the first horse to win the Triple Crown. A Triple Crown winner must win the Kentucky Derby, the Preakness Stakes, and the Belmont Stakes. Since the series began in 1875, no horse had won all three races. Jockey John Loftus rode Sir Barton to victory in the previous two races and was the winning jockey in the Belmont Stakes.

Sir Barton

INDEX

All over the United States, people celebrated Armistice Day with parades and parties. This jubilant crowd is marching up Fifth Avenue in New York City. 47